MERCED ABC 123

By Susan Walsh, Ed.D.

Dedicated to children who want to read
and to the organizations and individuals
who keep Merced beautiful.

All photos in **Merced ABC 123**
were taken in Merced California
by Dr. Susan Walsh.

ISBN: 9798351946115

Published in 2022 by Susan Walsh / Walsh, Cassady, & Walsh
The fifth book in the series: Solving Problems Through Literacy.

Letters of the Alphabet

A a	B b	C c
D d	E e	F f
G g	H h	I i
J j	K k	L l
M m	N n	O o
P p	Q q	R r
S s	T t	U u
V v	W w	X X
Y y	Z z	

A
is for
Ambulance.

Emergency Room Ambulance Entrance. 3600 Mercy Avenue.

B
is for
Boys & Girls Club.

Boys & Girls Club of Merced County, 615 W. 15th Street.

C
is for
Creek.

Bear Creek at E.S. Bear Creek Drive + Cameron Lane.

D

is for

Downtown.

Main Street between Canal and "K" Streets.

E
is for
Elks Lodge.

Merced Elks Lodge #1240. 1910 "M" Street.

F

is for

Fountain.

Laura's Fountain. "M" Street at 27th Street.

G

is for

Gazebo.

Applegate Park. 1045 W. 25th Street.

H

is for

Hospital.

Dignity Health Mercy Medical Center. 333 Mercy Avenue.

I

is for

Inn.

Bear Creek Inn. 575 W. N. Bear Creek Drive.

J

is for

Jet.

Merced Regional Airport. 20 Macready Drive.

K

is for

Kiddieland.

Kiwanis Kiddieland Amusement Center. 25 "O" Street.

L
is for
Library.

Children's Room. Merced County Library. 2100 "O" Street.

M
is for
Museum.

Merced Courthouse Museum. W. 21st & N Streets.

N

is for

Neighborhood.

Ragsdale Historic District. E. 26th Street.

O is for Overpass.

G Street Railroad Overpass. 25th & G Streets.

P

is for

Park.

Stephen Leonard Park. 640 T Street.

Q

is for

Quilts.

Gateway Quilters' Guild display. Civic Center.687 W. 18th Street.

R is for Roses.

Merced Rose Garden. "M" Street at 27th Street.

S

is for

Statue.

Unity Statue. Merced Civic Center. 678 W. 18th Street.

T
is for
Theatre.

Merced Theatre. 301 W. Main Street.

U

is for

University.

University of California Merced. 5200 N. Lake Road.

V
is for
Veterans.

Merced County Veterans Memorial. "M" & 21st Streets.

W
is for
Window.

Second Time Around Bookstore Display Window. 524 W. Main Street.

X
is for
X Street.

"X" Street intersection. Highway 140 and "X" Street.

Y

is for

Youth Sports Complex.

Nannini Youth Sports Complex. 1800 Wardrobe Avenue.

Z

is for

Zoo.

Applegate Park Zoo. 1045 W. 25th Street.

Numbers 1 to 10

1	One
2	Two
3	Three
4	Four
5	Five
6	Six
7	Seven
8	Eight
9	Nine
10	Ten

1

one

Tortoise

Merced Zoo Tortoise

2
two
Benches

Applegate Park Benches

3
three
Bears

Merced County Fair Bears

4
four
Roses

Phil Wilson's Roses

5

five

Columns

Mondo Building Columns

6

six

Books

Merced County Library Children's Books

7
seven
Windows

Windows in Small Barn, Merced County Fair

8
eight
Cookies

MIX Bakery Cookies

9

nine

Baseballs

Eric Nelson's Baseballs

10
ten
Peaches

McMillan Family Peaches

MERCED COUNTY OFFICE OF EDUCATION
HEY YOU!
DADA
YUM

Thank You

Darlene Nelson, Kathy Hailey,
Alissa Haynes, Cindee Prader,
Cathy and Mike McMillan,
Eric Nelson, Carolyn Vara,
Hub and Rita Walsh,
Phyllis Boyle, Stephanie Nelson,
Manuel Costa, Friedhelm Golz.

www.ingramcontent.com/pod-product-compliance
Lightning Source LLC
LaVergne TN
LVHW071127160826
845679LV00005B/1205
* 9 7 9 8 3 5 1 9 4 6 1 1 5 *